LOVE CAT

LOVE CATS

Your Favorite Cat Photo!

What
is
Your Cat's Name?

1. ZIRCON 2. CONCRETE 3. RED
4. WHITE 5. YELLOW GREEN

love

What Do Cats Purr?
Where Your Cat Sleeps?

1. ORANGE   2. BIZARRE   3. GRAIN BROWN

4. WHITE   5. GREEN

Write a story
about your favorite cat!

LOVE CAT
Favorite Drawing

1. RAW SIENNA 2. WHITE 3. SPRING WOOD
4. CLINKER 5. YELLOW

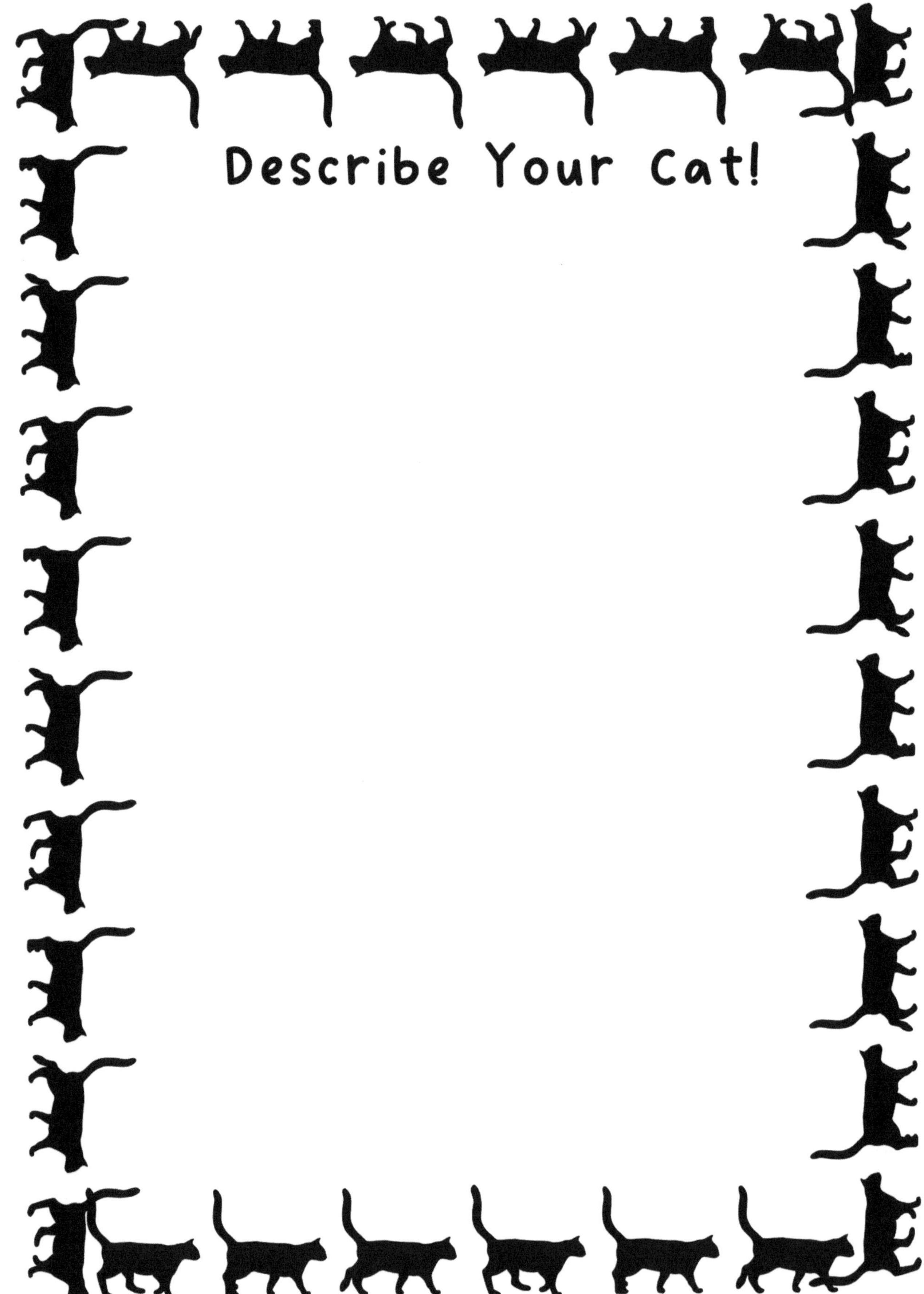

Describe Your Cat!

Me and My Cat

1. RED 2. MARSHLAND 3. PAARL 4. ORANGE
5. ORANGE 5. GREEN

Meow
LOVE
CATS

Your Favorite Drawing

1. BLACK 2. WHITE 3. TAHITI GOLD 4. TIDE
5. PORCELAIN 6. DESERT STORM 7. YELLOW

meow

1. BLACK   2. WHITE   3. WOOD
4. SPICY MIX   5. PEAR

My Cat

Be Creative and Enjoy Cats!

A Funny Photo

1. SPICE   2. SOFT AMBER   3. SANDRIFT

4. BEAVER   5. MY SIN

Your Happy Cat

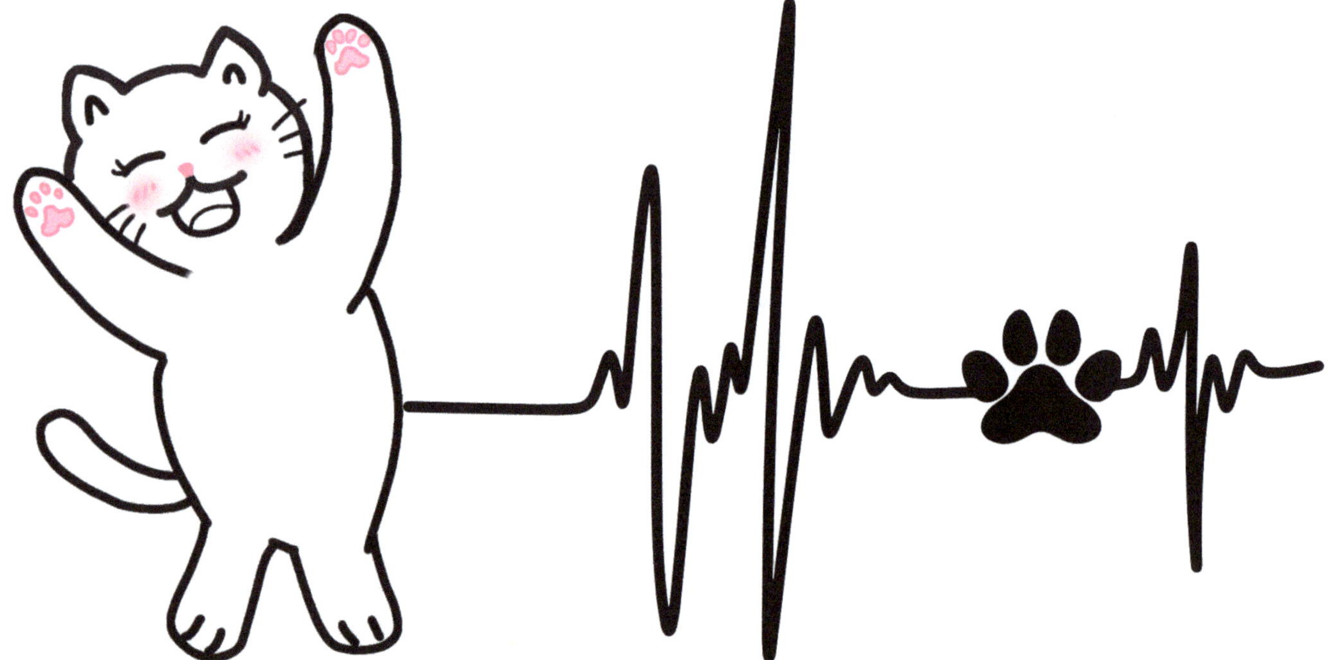

1. DUST STORM 2. CASHMERE 3. RAW SIENNA

4. WHITE 5. YELLOW

Your Cat is Lucky?

Your Favorite Drawing

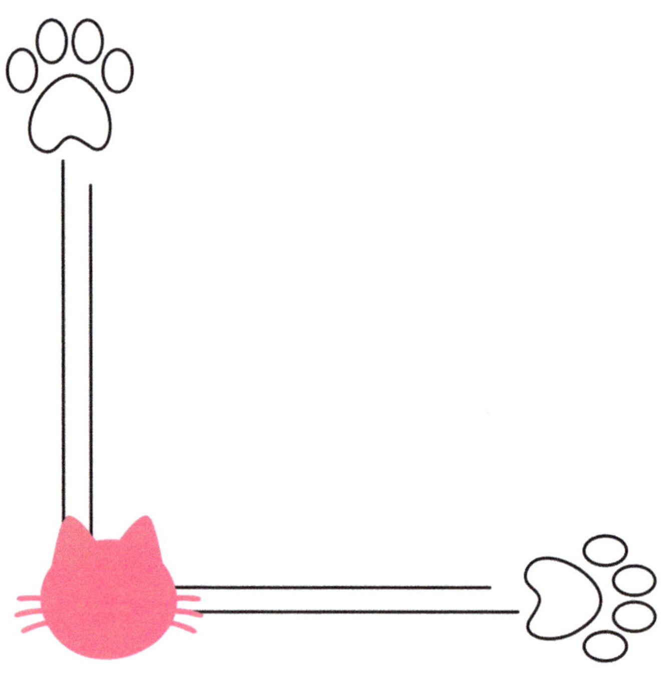

1. GRAIN BROWN   2. BIZARRE   3. KABUL

4. WHITE   5. GORSE

What's Your Cat Eating?

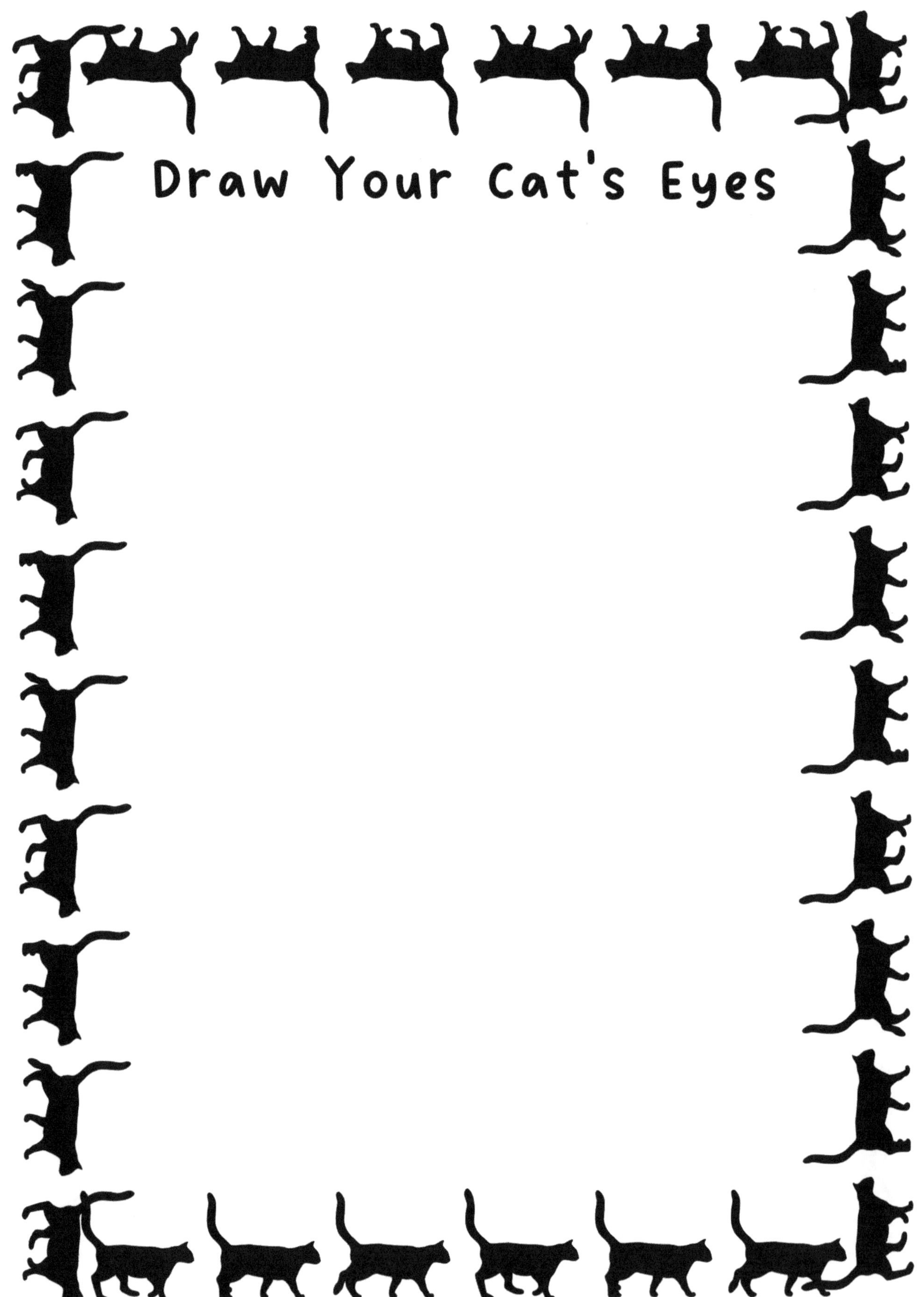

Draw Your Cat's Eyes

Meow

COLOR TEST PAGES

COLOR TEST PAGES

COLOR TEST PAGES

Thank you !

We would really appreciate your feedback, please send us a email to:

ritirra@gmail.com